The Stories of the

MoneyKind

Dedication

I dedicate the Stories of the MoneyKind to my gracious family; Ahmed, Sherif and Susana who always supported my project. And to my three gorgeous grandchildren Haroon, Nuria and Samir; my first fans. My friend Dalia and my mentor Penny Joelson believed in me and the MoneyKind. For that I'm ever so grateful.

Above all, the stories are profoundly dedicated to my dearest late son Shouhdi. He spent many hours of his short life on earth inventing the characters with me. I hope he's watching happily from heaven.

Fellows of the MoneyKind live a life parallel to that of humankind- similar in many ways but also unique. They have feelings, heads, arms, and legs, and can speak (even to humans if they choose).

This is one of their stories.

The Fez and the Turban Head

'Ha ha ha! What are you wearing on your head?' the Egyptian five-pound coin teased the American dollar coin, nicknamed Turban Head.

Turban Head wasn't pleased to have someone sneering at him, especially a coin wearing weirder headgear than his! 'What are you laughing at?' asked the annoyed Turban Head. 'Mind your own business. Instead of laughing at me, look at yourself and the odd headgear your wear!'

The Egyptian coin could not stop laughing. 'My headgear is famous. It's a fez that was worn by King Farouk, a previous ruler of Egypt'.

It was the first time the two coins had met, although they had lived in the same home for a while. Their home was a cabinet where Mr Amir kept his precious collection of coins in his luxurious house in New York City. Mr Amir had been a keen coin collector from a young age. When he was forced to leave his homeland of Iran many years before, he managed to take his collection with him. Every now and then, Mr Amir rearranged the coin display in the cabinet.

That day, he put the gold coins together in the big top drawer. 'I think I will place them here so that the guests will notice them when they come for dinner next week', he thought. 'I would like to see the looks of awe on their faces. Gold never fails to dazzle'. He smiled while arranging the coins.

Mr Amir placed the Egyptian five pounds so it was facing the Turban Head. Near them, he put a big gold coin from Zimbabwe. Around these three big coins, he scattered a few small gold commemorative coins issued only once for keen collectors.

The Zimbabwean coin was watching the two and didn't like the Egyptian coin's behaviour. The Zimbabwean coin said, 'It wasn't acceptable to sneer at Turban Head. You should say you are sorry'.

The Egyptian coin regretted his actions, so he apologised to Turban Head.

'But seriously, and I don't mean to offend, what's this strange headgear you are wearing?' he asked.

Turban Head sighed. 'It's not a turban. If you look carefully, it's the head of Liberty, the American symbol of freedom, wearing an ancient cap called a pileus'.

The Zimbabwean coin was listening, but he didn't seem to understand, 'What is a pileus?'

'A pileus is a Roman cap that was given to the slaves when they were freed. It's meant to stress the importance of liberty', replied the American coin.

The Egyptian coin turned his attention to the Zimbabwean coin. 'I hope you don't mind me asking. You carry a strange and long name. How do you say it?'

The Zimbabwean coin smiled. 'Mosi-Oa-Tunya is my name'.

'Wow, such a tongue twister', joked the Egyptian coin. The Zimbabwean coin smiled again.

'It's all right. You can call me Mosi. In fact, I'm named after the famous Victoria Falls in Africa. My name means "the smoke that thunders"'.

The Egyptian coin was about to comment, but Mosi quickly continued, 'Before you say smoke never thunders, I can tell you that our tribes gave it that name because of the sound the mist causes at the waterfalls'.

Mosi proudly showed the picture of the falls inscribed on his chest.

All the other coins surrounded Mosi to have a closer look. A small South African gold Rand with a picture of a hippopotamus on his body asked if he could touch the falls inscription.

An Australian Kangaroo gold coin spoke to the Egyptian coin.

'How about you, Egyptian fellow? Do you know anything about your origin?'

'Me? Of course I do', said the Egyptian coin. 'I

have a happy beginning. I was struck to celebrate a special occasion for my king, his marriage to his first wife, Safinaz, in 1938,' he said, as he showed off the date. 'Those were happy days before the divorce,' he sighed.

'But what was the cause of their separation?' asked Turban Head.

The Egyptian coin -who was always up for a joke- had a cunning thought, 'Why don't I play a game and try that Turban on? We could all have a laugh by swapping our head gear'. He looked at Turban Head smiling and nodded to his Turban, 'I will tell you if you swap your turban with me for a while, just for fun.'

Turban Head was hesitant but agreed because he was eager to know more about the story. He handed his turban to the Egyptian coin, took the fez and put it firmly on his head.

'That's much lighter!' he said. 'Now tell me, why did the king divorce the queen?'

The Egyptian coin found it difficult at first to fit the turban on his head, but he managed to do it in the end. 'Oh, this is rather loose and doesn't fit me', he said before continuing his story. 'King Farouk needed to have an heir to the throne, but Queen Farida only bore him girls, so he married again to secure a baby boy'.

Mosi, who was following the chat, interrupted the Egyptian coin. 'Wait a minute. I thought the queen was called Safinaz'.

The Egyptian coin laughed. 'Well spotted Mosi. Yes. That was her real name', he said. 'But the royal tradition in Egypt was that members of the royal family should bear the same initials, so she changed her name to Farida to match the king's name, Farouk'.

Turban Head was beginning to like the fez. 'I really like it. Do you know what it is made of?'

'It's made of felt, cheap compared to the silk material your turban is made of,' the Egyptian coin replied. He was beginning to feel hot under the turban, which needed a lot of adjustment, and was starting to regret the swap as it didn't cause the laughable reaction he expected from other coins.

'Maybe we better swap the headgear now; the fez does not really suit you'. He said.

'No, I'd like to keep the fez on for a while', replied Turban Head as he ran his fingers over the fez. 'It must have been fun to wear such a light cap in summer',

But the Egyptian coin was getting annoyed and demanded to have his fez back. He took off the turban and put it aside. 'It feels so warm in your turban. Can I have my fez back now?'

Turban Head didn't want to return it. 'Not until you tell me a bit more about it. Did the fez originally come from Egypt?'

'No, it's Moroccan. It was invented in a town named Fez; now, will you return it?' requested the Egyptian five pounds.

Turban Head ignored the request. 'But if it originated in Morocco, how come you used to wear it in Egypt?'

The Egyptian coin became angry.

'Look, I'm not answering any more questions until you give me my fez', he shouted.

The other coins in the drawer stood back, watching the argument between the two coins.

Mosi tried to calm the situation.

'Look my Egyptian friend, you've had the fez all these years; why don't you leave it to Turban Head to enjoy for tonight?' he suggested. The other coins agreed. So, the Egyptian coin unwillingly accepted.

The next morning, Turban Head didn't want to give the fez back. The Egyptian coin complained to other coins in the drawer.

'You can be generous and leave the fez with him for a few days', said the Australian Kangaroo coin.

'It will show how considerate you are'.

More days passed, and still, Turban Head didn't want to return the fez; meanwhile, the Egyptian coin refused to wear the turban.

'It's heavy, big and loose', he said to the coins. 'I want my fez back'.

But he never got it. The atmosphere in the drawer became hostile because of the clash between the two coins. The coins were divided about the issue. Some thought the fez should be returned, while others didn't mind the change of the headgear. The Egyptian coin was so upset, he threatened to tell Mr Amir when he next opens the drawer.

'Please don't do that', begged an Austrian gold coin with musical instruments. 'If Mr Amir knows about this problem, he will send us back to our different drawers. And in my drawer, I'm the only gold coin among coins of copper and nickel. They are always bullying me'.

The Egyptian coin didn't know what to do! He felt sorry for the Austrian coin and didn't want to upset her, but in the meantime, he blamed himself. 'I wanted to play a joke on Turban coin but the joke is now on me. He sat sulking in a corner and didn't speak to anyone.

A few days before the dinner invitation, Mr Amir decided to check his coin collection before the guests arrived. When he opened the drawer, he was shocked.

'What happened here to my two most precious coins, Turban Head and the Egyptian five pounds?' He gasped. 'Jumbled headgear! And what do we have here? Turban Head is wearing the fez? And what is the turban doing there on the drawer?'

Mr Amir thought thieves had broken into his house and replaced the real coins with fake ones. He immediately called the police.

'My house has been burgled', he said, 'and my most precious coins have been tampered with!'

A policewoman accompanied by a colleague arrived and inspected the room, the cabinet and the house thoroughly but found no trace of a break-in.

'We believe the thieves are from inside the house', the policewoman said. 'We are going to question everyone who works here.'

The coins were alarmed at what they heard. Mosi thought it wasn't right to have an innocent person accused of theft or tampering with the coins.

'We need to sort this matter out among ourselves before someone gets punished', he whispered to the other coins. The Austrian gold coin mumbled quietly. 'Please, remember my problem and the bullies in my drawer. We can't discuss this issue in front of everyone. We'll do it when the police have gone'.

Overnight, the coins gathered to debate the problem and seek a solution. A Chinese gold coin with an inscribed panda started talking first: 'I believe that one can't munch another person's bamboo. So, Turban Head should give the fez back'.

Tiger gold coin disagreed. 'The Egyptian coin is at fault. Why did he give up his fez in the first place? He should keep the turban', he snarled.

The Egyptian coin protested, 'But I only lent the fez to Turban Head for fun. That doesn't mean he can keep it.'

The Austrian gold coin said, 'I think we were wrong to stay silent when Turban Head refused to return the fez. 'Borrowing something doesn't mean you hold onto it forever'.

Mosi listened in silence for a while before speaking: 'The police are returning in the morning to continue their investigation. So, let's take a vote. Who agrees that the fez is to be returned?'

All the coins voted for returning the fez except Tiger gold coin, so Mosi announced, 'Only one coin disagrees, so we ask Turban Head to give the fez back to the Egyptian coin'.

Turban Head was upset to take off the fez and return it. He reluctantly put the turban on and sat, annoyed in a corner by himself. The Egyptian coin was sorry to see him sad. He squatted next to Turban Head, 'Don't be upset fellow. You wouldn't like someone to be falsely accused of theft, he said. 'Besides, the turban suits you better; it matches the liberty figure you carry'.

Before going to sleep, the Egyptian coin was pleased as he adjusted the fez on his head. 'I didn't appreciate the value of my fez until I almost lost it,' he thought.

The following day, Mr Amir opened the cabinet to check on the coins before the police arrived. To his surprise, he found all the gold coins safe and normal.

Turban Head was wearing his turban, and the fez was fitting perfectly on the head of the Egyptian coin. After examining the coins thoroughly, he called the police and apologised. 'I don't know what had happened, but all my coins are fine this morning. I don't have an explanation. There must have been a mistake'. He said as he closed the cabinet.

And to this day, Mr Amir has never understood how he came to find his coins with jumbled headgear as the gold coins kept it as a secret. The Austrian gold coin was grateful for the other coins who helped her to stay away from the drawer with the coins who gave her trouble.

And That's The End of The Story

Printed in Great Britain
by Amazon

28086707R00016